Barnesville Pumpkin Festival Yearbook 2021

I would like to thank all of you who contributed photographs for this book.

If I forgot or missed a photo that you sent me, I apologize.

Copies of this book are available at Blossoms Flower Shop and at the Chamber of Commerce office in downtown Barnesville. They are also available on Amazon.com

mikeduve@gmail.com   740-213-3789

Barnesville Pumpkin Festival Yearbook 2021

© 2021 Michael Duve all rights reserved.

2021

Barnesville Welcomes The Return Of The

Pumpkin Festival

**Another Record Setting King Pumpkin.
Grown by Jeff Theil of Dillonvale, Ohio.**

It was a cold wet start to the festival on Wednesday night.

The weather was perfect for the Big Parade on Saturday. With Grand Marshal Reed Tychonski and featuring Marching Bands from Barnesville, Bellaire and St. Clairsville.

2020 Pumpkins the Year without a Festival.